Fabulous Beast

Dear Rosemary,
    It was a pleasure meeting
you at Indie Author Day at
the Herndon Fortnightly Library!
I look forward to reading your
dog mystery novella, :)
particularly as a fellow dog
lover.
    Best of luck w/ your
writing & publishing.
            Sarah

FABULOUS BEAST

poems

sarah kain gutowski

Texas Review Press • Huntsville

Library of Congress Cataloging-in-Publication Data

Names: Gutowski, Sarah Kain, author.
Title: Fabulous beast : poems / by Sarah Kain Gutowski.
Description: Huntsville, Texas : Texas Review Press, [2019] |
Identifiers: LCCN 2019011573 (print) | LCCN 2019014964 (ebook) |
ISBN 9781680031997 (eBook) | ISBN 9781680031898 |
ISBN 9781680031898(pbk. : alk. paper)
Subjects: LCSH: Women—Poetry. | Mothers—Poetry.
| LCGFT: Poetry.
Classification: LCC PS3607.U85 (ebook) |
LCC PS3607.U85 A6 2019 (print) | DDC 811/.6—dc23
LC record available at https://lccn.loc.gov/2019011573

Cover art: *CY*, ink jet print, © 2015, Ellen Garvins

The bud
stands for all things,
even for those things that don't flower,
for everything flowers, from within, of self-blessing;
though sometimes it is necessary
to reteach a thing its loveliness,
to put a hand on its brow
of the flower
and retell it in words and in touch
it is lovely
until it flowers again from within, of self-blessing.

  —Galway Kinnell, "Saint Francis and the Sow"

The Chimera was more fearful than a nightmare. . . .
She spat fire from all her three heads . . .

    —Ingri and Edgar Parin D'Aulaire,
    D'Aulaires' *Book of Greek Myths*

CONTENTS

CONTENTS

The cicadas chirr in the dark trees. Their collective noise builds, a wave coming ashore, and breaks against the screen of my daughter's open window, flattening into a lower register. We adjust the pillows. We read more myths, myths she inherits. They are full of words we learn together: *jotun, Aesir, Yggdrasil, Lidskjalf.* Our voices rise and fall as we recite them out loud: Hers is high and loud and trills like the crescendo of cicadas, and mine rumbles low, a wave receding. I relearn the way I pronounce *Odin: ooooo-din.* I stumble over *Ginunggagap.* Her questions rise and fall with my answers throughout our reading.—*Who is that girl?—Freya. She had a suit of falcon feathers. When she wore it she could fly.—Why did Odin hang himself?— He knew knowledge would make him powerful. He made a sacrifice to gain knowledge. Does that make sense to you?—Not really.* She stares at the illustrations, moves the book closer to her face.— *Loki had monsters for children?— He married a monster. So they had little monsters. He loves them, even though they're monstrous, right?— Right.* Our dog grumbles at the foot of the bed: between cicadas and her questions, he cannot sleep.—*Did all of this really happen?* The cicadas hum their refrain.—*A long, long time ago, people used stories to explain the world around them. When their daughters asked, How was the earth made? they answered, From the body of a fallen giant. And when they asked, why do the sun and moon rise and disappear each day? they answered, Because a pack of wolves chase them across the sky.* My daughter thinks about this.—*Do we use stories to explain things now?* She yawns. I close the book.—*Sometimes.*

1. The Sow

The Mother Moves in the Dark

Depending on where she throws her weight,
the sow may or may not create the dead,
rolling over her young and crushing them.

She has so little control over the great body
she wakes inside, with a groan, each morning.
Such a burden: to be locked in flesh.
Her breast hangs down in one long line of teat,
a nipple for each hungry mouth.

She is used to being used, and knows—
with wisdom passed down from animal to animal,
beast to beast, mother to daughter, and even father to son—
a greater slaughter waits than this one.

The Mother Cannot Ask for
What She Needs

Usually the sow sleeps solidly,
head flat to the earth, listening to the grubs
and beetles move. Nothing can wake her.

But sometimes a scent or a sound pulls her
from the dreamless mud. She shuffles
into the garden's black air:she looks up,
and she loves the cool scent of honeysuckle
awakened at night; she loves not her odorous, thick hide
but the earth that sings under her cloven feet.

Against the darkness, she feels like a sponge:
she waits to be emptied, so she can fill up again.

The Mother Shifts Her Shape

She can change at will,
and sometimes against her will:
Most of the time she is the sow,
muscular but not easily moved;

then the sky turns the sick green color
of an approaching storm in summer,
or the farmer's alarm clock chirrups
at the wrong time, or the fire whistle
shatters her sleep.

Then, suddenly, she is a monkey
baring its hot gums and yellow teeth.
Or she is a nit, pestilent and blind,
sinking into someone's skin.

Poof!—she runs tumor-backed, a mouse in a maze.
Poof!—she kneels, mouth bloodied, over prey.
Poof!—the cold Atlantic beads on her head
as she leaves its roiling waves.

And each time the smoke clears she wonders:
For how long will she stay incarnate
in this new shape? For how long will she be
locked in a strange skin, married to an alien name?

The Mother Grows Tired of Excuses

It isn't metamorphosis that makes her a witch
so much as the malevolence that rises, her body
riding waves of heat. She abhors her lack of patience
with the piglet's teeth, her heavy sigh and the way
she lumbers just out of reach, as much as she loathes
in those same sharp moments the piglet's need,
its insistent nudge against her teat,
All she wishes for is blinding sun
unbroken by touch or squeal, warm earth
cushioned by darkest sleep, no matter
whether these interruptions speak
of want or the deepest natural love.

The Stories Our Mothers Use Against Us

When you were small, the sow begins,
*I brought you to a patch of dirt, dry and cool
under the crab apple tree. All around us,*
she tells her piglets, *the little birds fluttered
and covered their hot wings with the dust.*

*I rooted around the tree's trunk
and found knotted grubs and rocky fruit
for our lunch, while you all lay down,
little bellies flat against the ground,
and closed your eyes. Each one of you
claimed you felt the world spinning.*

*Eventually I ceased my efforts
to feed your twelve hungry mouths,
and I lay my dry body in the dust, too,
where I imagined I had wings to cover with dirt—
that I was pinned to the whirligig earth
not by the fact of my flesh and bone, but by choice.*

The Mother Makes Time for Herself

When her body does what she wants,
her cloven feet grow long and dexterous.
The splitting hurts, but the sow gives herself to this pain.

Newly formed she lets herself—now a girl, complete
with long, nimble fingers—into the farmer's house.
Then at the family piano, she sits because she can bend—
actually bend—at the waist. And she begins to play—
not with hesitation, but with all the energy surging
through this new female form. She pummels the keys
with her soft, smooth finger-pads: no noise!
Just each hammer hitting the strings like rays of light,
the pedals sighing and stretching clear, resonant notes.

The bellows in her heart pumps the music,
in and out, in and out—nothing nasal,
no braying or porcine grunt—and she plays
until she hears the farmer's step on the porch.

When he enters, he finds only a sow in his living room.
Distraught and wild over her sudden weight returned,
she fractures the piano stool, her hooves slam the keyboard,
and she falls to the wide wood planks of the floor.

Some Things the Mother Cannot Change

When she feels lonely and she envies the swan
her constant mate, the sow lumbers
into the moonlight and shifts her shape again
to resemble the widowed farmer's wife.

This body feels heavier than that of the girl
who played the piano with joy in the family room,
but it—she—his wife's ghost—is no less
a moon beam or a pale dream that moves softly
through the farmhouse and into the marriage bed.

When she lifts the coverlet and nestles beside him,
naked and opulent, this is what she gives the farmer:
A dream. A walk through rows and rows of lavender.
And when she laces his calloused fingers with her own,
he loops his hands through the lattice of a rope swing,
and sails back and forth over a generous, bright river.
The sun warms his face whenever she sighs.

And when he breathes into her, his sow-wife, she smells the
    earth,
freshly disturbed and wet with life. His kiss tastes
hot and peppery, like roots or vegetables harvested too soon.

The Stories Our Mothers Teach Us

for Lisbeth and Nikolina

When I was your size and just weaned,
the sow tells her piglet,
I found a hole in our pen and squeezed
my small, round body through.

At first, no one missed me. I ran across the farmer's fields,
slipped into a ditch filled with nettle and wire,
and then climbed out, skin and snout torn.
Between the edge of the field and that stinging, tearing abyss
I sat, panting at the sky. All the stars tapped and telegraphed
shiny, tinny warnings, but I refused to listen.

The night wind smelled sharp with burning wood
and honeysuckle,and I had to follow the scent.
That was the day I fell in love with blindness,
and the strange way that scent, and even stench,
can comfort us. But I was found, and now I have scars.

May I go into the woods one day? her piglet asks.
It is my duty to deny, the sow says.
Your duty is to listen, and then dig
and dig under fences at night.

The Threats Our Mothers Pose

Suddenly and separate from her shape-shifting,
the sow grows one more row of teeth
like those of a shark, planes sharp and weak
as obsidian flake but colored a creamy pearl.

Blood skirts her gums where each new tooth
needled through, and collects in the crevices
of her older, worn molars. She doesn't know
what to think. Her teeth are apt to fall out
when she opens her mouth to speak, or to chew.

And when they do, from the root of her jaw
sprouts another slant dagger, and her children
turn their triangular heads and blink their eyes
whenever she grins. The teeth are a gypsy curse
if her shape-shifting is God's blessing.

And yet she finds comfort in her tongue
resting against those points and fangs,
and the way she shudders whenever she catches,
in the water trough, her newly profaned image.

The Mistakes Our Mothers Make

I birthed my first litter in another field like this.
From where I'd built my nest, I could see
the horizon's edge glitter in the wet morning,
a spring rain cutting through the hard earth
and preparing it for the till.

I lay confused on my pallet of chewed grasses,
the twigs and leaves I'd crushed without knowing why,
or for what event, I prepared.

Birthing was less a miracle and more of a letting go,
the release of a knot I'd carried for months
within my belly. I didn't understand
the small, wet shapes that glistened under the early sun—
and their first sucks of air, their little hooves
kicking, silently, scared me.

When the farmer found me with afterbirth
hanging in a long drool from my jaw,
and only two piglets remained
from the six, he knew what I'd done.
He raised the leftover babies to my breast
and neither had to fight for food.

The sow grunts softly to the litter
that slides from her now, slipping,
each a water drop from a rain-soaked leaf.

Your luck is not real luck, she sings to them.
My darlings, you will grow lousy with it.

What Our Mothers Know as Love

The sow watches the farmer apply grease to her son,
a young boar with a wound long and thin where he rubbed
    himself
clean of bristles and skin. This itch belongs to more than just
    disease
and parasites. She recognizes the anxiety foaming on his chin;
knows that his panic has been growing since the males were
    confined
to a pen, and shuttered away from the sows in the field.

Only half-grown, and he carries his weight like a club.
His short tusks bruise the farmer's hand when he bucks in
    protest.
For days he's rubbed his back along the splintered rail,
    cutting a slender flap
in his hide—an open envelope that invites infection. Though
    half blind,
his mother sees the fear leaping from him in flecks of foam:

it is more than a squeal ringing in her ears, it is a throbbing
    in her gut,
a pulse that makes her run back and forth, wailing. She calls
from the other side of the fence, even though he was weaned
    weeks ago,
and she let the boy wander from her side, as if she no longer
    needed him.

The Reason Our Mothers Can't Help Us

Most days, the sow's disinterest in her children confounds her.
She watches the cattle stay close to their offspring,
walking and grazing side by side, for most of their lives.
She cannot remember saying goodbye
to any of her own. One day they were attached to her teats,
sleeping in her shadow, and the next they wandered
beyond the pen's cement apron, and her view.

They disappeared. As if they shifted shape, too,
each a young pig morphing into a bird
and lifting into the air until the sky turned dark.
Perhaps she walked under that mottled canopy,
wondering where one or two of them were,
or why her breast felt full and without relief.

The sow senses there is a different way to be
about one's young. The swan would say so—and the horse.
A murder of crows blacks the air,
and each beat of their wings scolds her.

Our Mothers Are Children, Too

There is a place inside the sow that mourns
the loss of her own mother. Like garlic turning black and
    acerbic
inside its pale skin, the place housing her memories darkens
to a fresh bruise. With difficulty she remembers
the one who birthed her—a figure made from fog
rising off the yellowed grass on a hot August morning.

The steam of that sow's breath clouds her head now,
the only part of her mother that lingers.
She can no more fault her mother than she can the farmer,
who, in his way, and by turn, fathers and husbands her.

I loved my mother, I love my mother, she sings,
when—of all things—she lays in the concrete sty nursing
her newest litter of children. She listens to their song in
    response,
their grunts and whistled, nasal inhalations. Together,
mother and offspring, they are a satisfied chorus paying
    homage
to the necessity of the parent, and the necessity of what is,
    also, absent.

What Loves Us Also Kills Us

Perhaps no lesson is simpler than this.
The sow learns the sum of her life:
the farmer's hand, which guided her so swiftly
from the warmest bed, her mother's body,
will be the same hand to sell her with a handshake
or render her to meat.

While she breathes she is the animal he loves,
and the means by which he gains more pigs, more meat.
She recognizes she will always be food, a source of
    sustenance,
no matter how many times she finds herself changing.

As easily as she would nurse another sow's young,
she will give her womb, her blood and her bile,
to the farmer's purposes. He is the reason she exists.

Why a Mother Doesn't Fight Back

The sow recognizes defeat. She feels it first
in her submission to farrowing,
when there is nothing left to do but lie down in the dirt
and give in to muscles that act with or without her consent.

She knows it for the squeal from her runt,
who noses the weaker teats near her back legs,
and never finds the milk that satisfies.

She knows it for the look in the farmer's eyes
when frost crawls into the crops he rendered,
so patiently, from the cruel ground.

And she feels it, a warm and growing pool under her feet,
when the farmer finally takes his knife
and she becomes a body without breath,
another carcass without heat.

Where Have We Taken Our Husbands and Fathers?

When the boar is brought to serve the sow,
she understands that she is there to teach him;
that in this life, this form, there are few instincts
left to be trusted.

The male does not know he is male
or what his purpose may be
until he has been guided and soothed,
and treated tenderly. He must be told he is good,
that what he does is work, and blesséd work,
sanctioned by the farmer's firm insistence,
that voice always hovering in the background.

The boar cannot imagine in that moment
the act's importance, or how his performance,
to which he gives himself readily,
will suffer in a short, hurried season.

And he does not consider then, how he will suffer,
dragged by his most natural and unguarded parts,
to be hung for any cold eye to see, his spilled gut
a map the world reads to guide itself onward.

Why Our Mothers Panic

Some days, even the walls of the field are too much for the sow.
Holes in the fence taunt her. Once upon a time she fit
      through,
and could run to wide, bright fields where grass escaped
from livestock and the earth sat flat, untilled by the tractor.

Her own hunger increases on days like this,
when she feels trapped by clouds capping the sky,
or the relentless pull from piglets suckling,
or the indifferent look from the farmer, who brings her
      dinner.

On days like this, her head is not a skull filled with net-
      worked matter,
its own system of fences and walls built up and torn down
      over time.
It is an empty cavern sleeved with hanging bats, who bide
until the darkness ripples outward,waves of changing light
or sound that roust them into flying away.

Then, her thoughts are a mad confusion of wings.

Why Our Mothers Never Age

The sow cannot count her years by litters or seasons,
nor her days by sunsets or the shadow's crawl across the sky.
The timer inside her runs down heartbeats, not minutes,
and keeps her inhalations steady, moves her heavy limbs
to rise at dawn and receive the farmer's call.

She has always been this age, walking from pen to field
and back without hesitation or regret,
because an animal kept by routine rarely pauses
from fear or sorrow. Each day begins gray
and rendered by broad strokes, the color of uncooked fat,
then shrinks and solidifies with the day's heat.

The long hash marks on the fence rail
are not a catalog of days, but mark a rare freak
occurrence: the moment and the place
where her teeth could not, or would not, break through.

How Our Mothers Deal with Pain

The strangest parts of being a woman begin at night:
the moon half eclipsed by someone else's shadow
and warmed to red with refracted light. She can see
the farmer's hand reach for her, the sow transformed
to a wife's shape, and she rides the undercurrent of his need
until he moves like a cloud across her view.

In the dark her pain surprises her,
not from his weight or his tender breach
but from deep inside, where a satellite has lost its orbit,
and the blood that rings the sheets just below her human legs
looks much the same as the blood that will drop,
almost unnoticed, between the rivulets of mud in the pen.

No matter her form, woman or sow,
she is always surprised by the cycle's ache,
her body's dull routine, if only for the minutes it takes
for the farmer's silhouette to sink back into the bed
and return her view of the moon, which releases
its red hue and casts away the earth's shadow.
And now there's blood on the bed, and laundry to be done,
and no time to dwell on a throb or cramp in her womb.
Above them, the moon spins but doesn't appear to move.

Why Our Mothers Wish Us to Be Quiet

When voices, animal and machine, rise together and lodge in
    her ears
like driftwood spikes on a wave-worn beach, and cicadas
    grate
with their frantic, rising call, the sow's heart shuts down.

All of its lights go off, and for seconds it bobs on the tide of
    her breath.
Now she is deaf as well as blind, and this is another type of
    shifting,
a shape surrounded by watery shadows and an alien, neon
    glow.

She hears nothing but feels the sea's roar,
miles of pressure pounding her head.
Submerged like this, she steers herself toward deeper calm.

How Our Mothers Keep Moving

Shifting from one animal to another, having to grow easy
with new skin, more eyes, fewer legs,
and a center of gravity low to the earth
or tottering high above its spring-soaked plains,
brings exhaustion:

when the sow returns to her familiar, fattened body
she exhales a low, wordless song. Her children run to her,
eager to be familiar again with the parts they need.

They suckle and listen to her heartbeat, its rhythm slowing
until it is matched with their mouths, a steady music
they know and love, that sings to them: *stay with me.*

And while they grunt, the sow allows herself
to relax her own legs, to close her own eyes, and shift
not into another body or shape but into sleep and dream.
Her sleeping life is without sound or movement:
just a blindness and the faint smell of rotting vegetation.

When she wakes, startled by her child's cry,
she remembers nothing.

What Our Mothers Won't Name

How much wisdom has this shifting brought her?
At dawn, or at sun down, or high noon or midnight,
she is still the same dumb creature,
silent with her lack of correctness, the right language,
smart enough to recognize where she has failed
to enact the lessons of experience, despite their magic.
What use is transformation if it sits unused
in the atlas of the brain, growing outdated
as the world it represents breaks and reforms
again and again, with a purpose she senses
but cannot comprehend, beyond recognition?

The sow retreats into prostrate sulks
and the cramp of sleep, for what else can she feel
when she catches her reflection in the trough,
after seeing so many ways to live
in the world, and yet always returning
to the same, mute immovable bulk,
the same creature who will be acted upon,
and consumed, and consumed, and finally consumed?

There was always a hole in the fence
or sudden wings, strange but workable
extending from her spine, and an expanse of sky
or a sheltering forest waving its many invitations;
she could have left and yet she stayed,
she could have morphed but she remains
essentially unchanged, tongue thick in her mouth,

legs bent, her weight fixed to this spot,
this dent in the earth, this corner of air
in the stagnant yard, where she lies
while the flies build their kingdoms
along the hills and valleys of her hide.

How Our Mothers Recognize Their Limits

for Joshua

One night when the sow lies next to the farmer, but in his dead
    wife's shape,
she hears their son, crying from his bed. The body she inhabits
    moves
in response, and she glides over the rough farmhouse floor-
    boards
as easily as if she slid across a frozen lake. When she reaches
    the boy,
his legs half off the bed and exposed to the night air, something
    loosens inside her.

Like a shelf of snow too heavy for its tree limb,
she feels a piece of her second self fall away, the one who
    birthed her young
because she woke one morning with children growing inside her,
and that is what female pigs do: give birth, give birth, give birth,
then give up when the farm's machine decides she has given
    enough.

She raises the boy and drapes him over this other female's
    shoulder,
in a way she could never lift her own young with the sow's
    awkward body.
He breathes clouds into the air beside her head, and that vapor
    mixes
with her own exhalations. Together they sway, boy and his ghost
    mother,
winter whistling through the eaves above his bed.

2. The Woman with the Frog Tongue

Chapter I: She Leaves Home
(Absention)

A long time ago, and very far away,
    a little girl began to speak with the language of birds
    and insects. Even when she cried her sobs were thin,
    brittle: the pitch of bats, sporadic as cricket song.
    Her laughter flew around the room like a frantic lark
    trapped inside four walls. And how she loved to talk!
    There came a rising in her chest, a sudden impulse
    to comment she couldn't check. Compulsory as breath,
this music was a measure her body dared not work against.

After a while, her parents, neighbors, and family friends—
    they all tried to suppress her endless chatter. *Stop,*
    they'd reprimand, *stop talking.* Nothing dammed the noise
    cascading from her mouth, however—not the doctor,
    who peered into her throat's dark recess and hoped to find
    some rare illness sat within; and not the priest,
    who searched her heart and head through prayer, and yet
      could not
    expel the demon working there, the devil cupped
inside her tender soul. He declared her lost, her cause
    annulled.

Everyone had given up. She recognized
    defeat in her father's face, and knew she'd drained his
      patience.
    Her mother trembled with frustration. So she left,
    a girl no longer, but a woman young and filled
    with dread at what she might encounter in the world.
    She shuffled down the road, its tar face flat and silent.
    Sometimes she'd stop to chat with catbirds on a fence,
    or join an open field's frenetic nighttime riot,
but she was often alone, and growing very sad and quiet.

Chapter II: She is Warned, and Ignores the Warning
(Interdiction and Violation)

I.

One day, her gut swollen with sounds she hadn't voiced,
    she stopped to read a sign hanging above a door.
    Come in, come in, the healer coughed at the shadow she made,
    and since he was the first person who'd spoken to her
    for many weeks, she entered. There in a dim room
    a hobgoblin sat: his hair oak-dark, his limbs gnarled
    like thick tree roots. She stood still at the door and sang,
    the creature sounds riding her ragged breath. *It's a curse,*
she spoke in birdsong. *I cannot form their words. What could be*
      worse?

The hobgoblin rubbed his knotted hands together and blew
    inside the nest they made, as if coaxing flame from tinder.
    Small sparks starred the darkness, followed by clouds of
      smoke
    that filled the room, their long, dense plumes coming apart
    like drafts from a signal fire. She waved away the fog,
    and moved closer. He touched her lips with warm fingers.
    Speak, he urged. She opened her mouth and out flew bees
    and hummingbirds, wasps and crows, a swarm of katydids,
an elf owl, beetles, moths, and swallows—and last—a lonely
      finch.

The abandoned branch of her throat felt sore. Her tongue began
    to swell and stretch, growing beyond her lips and teeth,
    until she couldn't hold it back. Unleashed, it fell
    and lolled across the floor, sticky and gathering dust.
    The little man laughed coarsely and rolled the dark, long
      muscle

from tip to root like carpet. He tucked it inside her mouth
   and helped her close her jaw. Then he pointed to the door.
   Now mute and choked by silence, she turned and walked
      away.
She coughed and spluttered down the road, alone once again.

II.

Unable to speak, and full of sorrow, the woman walked
   until—overcome, exhausted—her feet dragged to a stop.
   Above the trees she saw a tower's gilded turret
   The old, familiar rising in her belly told her:
   This is home. So she made her way through thorns and brush
   until she came to a door at the tower's base. She knocked.
   The door, unlocked, swung open. Up the cramped stairs
   she pulled herself, her head tilted to keep her tongue
inside the cage of her mouth. Her jaw ached from restraining
      its bulk.

She entered the tower's one round room, the kind of place
   where she, a woman newly changed and worn threadbare,
   could lay her body down and rest. On the large round bed
   a skein of silk and a ladder, roped around the bedpost,
   remained—a futile effort made by the last girl here.
   Atop a table beside the bed, a silver knife
   glinted next to a slender needle carved from stone.
   Robust vines clung to the window sash, invading the room.
Their leaves ticked softly against the walls. The air was damp
      and cool.

She perched on the bed, and sensed her tongue's desire to slide
   past her teeth and down to the cold marble floor.

It pulsed behind her lips—an animal testing its cage.
She held the needle to a beam of light and watched
the dust motes drift around and skirt the fine, sharp point.
Then she stitched the silken floss across her mouth until
a lattice formed through which water and air could slip.
White and clean as bone the needle worked her flesh.
The stitches were true and tight. She closed her eyes and tried
    to rest.

III.

After many days, a man approached the tower.
A prince. On errand, and weary from his search, he hoped
he might find rest within the tower's high room.
He climbed the stairs and when he saw the woman there
something inside his memory creaked, like cartilage
remembering how to work inside the knee again.
As if his life were a question and she, the calm reply,
he bent to take her answer. But when their lips touched
he felt the net of stitches: each thread tight, stiff, and cached in
    blood.

Something lived in there. He sensed it lurking, curled
and tense, preparing to strike. He pulled away, cobwebs
stuck to his teeth. The woman's eyelids flickered open.
She raised her head and stared into the prince's face,
handsome and scared, regret already written there
and mirroring her own, for they both knew he held
an empty promise in his kiss, and no solution.
She wiped the spider's silk from off his face. He left.
And there the woman stayed: her mind raging, her jaw clenched.

Mama, What Is Regret?

She misses her voice and its insect ring. The tower's emptiness
   tolls
waves of quiet, to the point where even her thoughts are mute,

and a series of pictures, not sounds, moves through her head.
The world moves around her. Every tossed tree limb,

every detached cobweb, whatever the wind shifts, speaks,
and it says to her: you were once this light, this moveable.

When she wakes from restless dreams and the stitches strain
between her lips, she feels more fully the reach of her silence.

She cannot even click or tsk her tongue in shame.
She has never felt so clumsy, so burdened and ungainly—

when she spoke with the black cricket's creak and whistle,
she knew someone, somewhere, understood her,

no matter if he was very small, and very slight, and likely to be
   crushed
between animal jaws or flattened under a human foot.

Even in her tower room, lying unencumbered on her bed, she
   sympathizes:
she feels it looming in the air above her, the force of that sud-
   den, obliterating weight.

Mama, How Does the Woman with the
  Frog Tongue Eat?

The regret she feels turns to rage, and with it the tenor of her
    dreams
changes, too: now she is a giant wave, an accumulation, a wet
    mouth

screaming toward the shore. She wants to devour it all,
beaches, trees, and grassy dunes. They disappear

beneath her massive overbite: Small towns, long roads,
the suburbs of cities and then the cities themselves.

She feeds the river and lake beds like a mother bird
who has chewed and digested food for her young,

and then they rise up, too, to devour the land and its
    inhabitants.
And then she is no longer water but a whale within it,

the detritus from felled and sea-scrubbed civilizations
    collecting
in her spiny teeth. She eats and eats: less to be full, more to
    destroy.

When she wakes, her jaw aches in the place where her
    molars ground together,
and her hunger is nothing but a nightmare: in daylight, less
    frightening, and gone.

Chapter III: She Cultivates a Harvest
She Cannot Reap
(Trickery and Deception)

She woke one morning to whispers, sounds entwined like
    threads,
    brushed along her outer ear. The feeling remained
    when, standing beside the tower's window, she scanned the
    mist
    floating above the trees and early summer grass.
    She followed the whispers down the tower steps until
    outside, and found a clearing. There, the world stopped
    its soft murmur and asked, distinctly, to be touched.
    In answer she bent and dug her hands into the earth,
tilling the soil until her fingernails were lined with dirt.

By noon her back ached and her forehead glistened with sweat.
    Her hands were blistered and marked with work's sheen, yet
    she sought
    more: a planting. She searched the forest for fallen fruit,
    their seeds, and roots she raised gently from dark, rich beds
    then cradled inside a sling she made with her long hair.
    Back in the clearing, she placed the seeds in tidy rows,
    built hills for the roots, and carried water cupped
    in her small palms to slake their thirst. She knew too well
the drought induced by change; everything had to be relearned.

The woman sheltered each tender and vulnerable sprout
    as if it were a human child stuck in the ground,
    thin new skin exposed to the sun, and little arms
    that waved to catch her attention. She hummed to them a lyric
    from when she was a child, when her mother's face loomed
    above her, large and cool as a moon that follows a day

of blistering heat. Her mother's voice, word after word,
   soaked into her dreaming life, so that now, by rote,
she sang it too, although only the melody left her throat.

This kind of mothering made her happy, briefly, until
   the season lengthened. Her plants rose tall above her head,
   dense and heavy with fruit of their own. She knew, too late,
   that what she'd grown had only grown to be eaten.
   Her lips, sewn together to hide her long, coiled tongue
   behind them, prevented even a taste. So back inside,
   she watched from her tower window's vantage the weeds riot
   unruly and thick between the rows. Her dry crop blanched,
and birds and rodents consumed the rotting fruit from dead
      branches.

Chapter IV: She Collects Objects That Are Not Hers
(Villainy)

In time, the silence and the nonsilence—her stifled breath,
    her furor without words—began to irritate
    like a hair, unseen, will torture the skin it hangs against.
    She wanted to rip it out. The empty, cold room
    amplified every noise until the walls rang.
    Beyond those walls, the landscape erupted with heat and rain,
    the season coaxing brambles into a green riot,
    a gloss of leaves from the trees, and roses wild with color.
She looked on them all without pleasure; they seemed crude
    and vulgar.

When she could no longer endure the nothingness
    rolling through her head, she ventured into the woods
    searching for objects that pleased her: silent, incapable
    of noise—like berries, bright and mute, reflecting not
    the sunshine nor her face in their dark bodies, but
    the bruised and burnished places housing her memories.
    She tramped through the forest, nettles caught inside her
        hair,
    and scalped the moss from trunks of trees. She lined her
        room
with these, her trophies, but they turned brown and brittle too
    soon.

Unable to bear her quiet room or the dead things
    littered across the floor, she left the tower again,
    but this time pressed beyond the woods to a nearby town.
    Its houses mottled the land with shadow, and from those
        homes
    came raucous laughter, high-pitched, volatile arguments,

and soft exchanges between lovers. Their noise made worse
the numb silence she dragged with her like a palsied limb;
she schemed to punish them by stealing objects they used
but left outdoors, on window sills or back porches or stoops.

She started small: ceramic dogs that guarded gates;
shingles felled by raging winds; a key untucked
from plastic, hollow stone; and various bubble wands
deserted or lost by children with fickle, careless hands.
Then larger items became her prey: gasoline cans,
lawnmower chains, old spades and rakes left leaning up
against a house, and pitchers of tea left out to sun.
She shuffled every stolen gadget and garden gnome
into the tower, until it was full and she felt less alone.

But with each passing day and item she'd collect,
her tongue would press more forcefully against the gate
she'd stitched across her mouth. Her stolen odds and ends
were safe inside the tower, and yet inside herself
a danger grew, a threat, although she couldn't say—
even inside her head, the place her voice remained—
exactly what or who it was she should protect.
She knew she felt more fear the more her corrupt mouth
    bulged.
If she clipped the last of its fraying strings, who knew what
    she'd become?

Chapter V: She Discovers What She Desires
(Lack)

I.

The woman felt her sadness most keenly at night,
    when voices raised together, ecstatic, and sang at once
    in varied tongues.She wished that she could answer back—
    instead, she sat among her collected baubles and watched
    their rough, skewed surfaces refuse the moon's dim light.
    The darkness, like sackcloth, rendered the room without color.
    She knew that somewhere within this clutter and junk
      there lay
    the splintered pole of her voice, which once upon a time
she might have used to vault from this quiet that left her
      unsatisfied.

And yet she heard in her head: *stop talking*, the old reproof.
    It cycled through her daily, a marble riding the slant
    rims of her mind and chiming against its many corners.
    This wasn't the noise she craved, and only when she tilted
    her head into her pillow did the torment roll
    to sudden, still silence. So she settled for sleep again,
    and rode its numbing waves through many nights and days,
    until she heard a child laughing, and woke from dream
while running to the window, her hands outstretched, as if she
      would leap.

The casement kept her from spilling down the tower's walls,
    even though she leaned over the sill and strained
    to hear the last notes that splintered her heavy slumber.
    The treetops swirled with reflected sun: a thousand leaves
    caught the light and threw back a refrain, like knives
    somersaulting toward her face: *too late, too late.*

But still, she clung to the sill and searched the canopy,
  as if a bird with a child's face lighted there and called
for others to sing with raucous laughter, too. The day grew long.

At last she gave up, and despaired of seeing the mouth
  or beak to blame for her broken sleep and manic watch.
  But just as the sun began its slow descent and dissolve
  behind the forest's vast, outstretched palm, two children
  marched through the brush and onto one of the narrow
    paths,
  hand in hand and homeward-bound, toward the village.
  They brandished walking sticks like spears, and their eyes
    were round
  and wide as shields, defense against the shapes that appeared
in mist and shadow along the trail. She recognized their fear.

They vanished beyond the tower's view, and even though
  the sun was setting, the woman ventured into the woods
  in search of where the children spent their day playing.
  At dusk, the trees on either side of the narrow path
  shook their spindle arms at her in shadowy clouds,
  leaves amassed like ghosts and rustling all around.
  Crickets evaded lizards along the forest floor,
  so the ground seethed and churned darkly beneath her feet.
Her brave resolve lifted away like fog. She made her retreat.

II.

The next morning she woke again to children's laughter.
  It traveled up the tower walls and ricocheted
  around her crowded room. When their baby voices argued

how best to find a way inside, she appeared above
specter-like, a waxen face without its body.
Startled, the children skittered into the brush like mice
suddenly raked by open air and a predator's gaze.
She hovered there, silent except for the whistling sounds
that only she could hear, that hastened past her cross-hatched
mouth.

She stood, a quiet, unmoving figure, until at last
the boy and girl scrambled from out of the shrubs and gazed
up at her face, back-lit by sun and blurred by that light.
Then the boy called, *Let down your hair*, and his sister
laughed.
She nodded toward the tower door, ajar, with stairs
visible just beyond. The boy and then the girl
picked up some stones, and hurled them through the door's
dark gap.
The stairs spat back an empty sound. The children looked up,
but she was gone. So they chucked their rocks at the window
ledge above.

A shriek of rusted metal hinges cut through the noise
of crag and pebble lobbed against the window pane.
They turned to see her standing close: her eyes bright,
her strange mouth webbed with string. She raised a hand in
greeting.
The girl's face broke from its brave smile. Her brother
ducked
under the heavy hail of stones they'd thrown overhead,
although one pierced the skin on his brow. With a cry, he ran.
His sister remained, her hand tracing the lines of her mouth –
testing the bars of its open gate, more curious than cowed.

Stumbling through the trees, the boy became aware
    he'd left his sister all alone with the strange woman.
    He doubled back, a red path working down his face.
    When he found the tower again the woman held a rag
    for him to take, and gave a tight, closed smile in welcome.
    The girl accepted, and pressed the scrap to her brother's
      head.
    Then she said, *We've made a fort inside the woods. A house.*
    It's where we play. Would you like to see it? Come with us.
She took the woman's fingers, still outstretched, and gently
      tugged.

Many years had passed for the girl who spoke like birds
    and insects, who grew to be this woman, frog-tongued –
    and many years since she'd heard a voice addressed to her,
    directly—so she felt wary, as if this child deceived,
    as if the girl were old enough to do her harm.
    The boy looked, too, like he couldn't quite believe his sister
    would make such a request of such a stranger, but
    she *had* offered the rag for his head, and she didn't seem
to want to do them harm. So he shrugged, and followed them
      through the trees.

III.

The children led her down the path to a small clearing,
    a patch of sun-bleached weeds eclipsed by a ring of trees.
    A dry creek ran through one corner, covered in part
    by sticks and vines woven together to make their fort.
    The woman felt exposed, crossing the field, like a doe
    that steps in front of the hunter's bow, aware of danger,
    but too palsied by fear to do more than stand and twitch.

In slow arcs, hawks drifted above their heads, while rabbits
hunkered between the tall, sheltering grasses, still as granite.

At the creek bed the children jumped over the edge
    where water should have lapped and dark clouds of guppies
    swirled inside a gentle current, but drought instead
    had licked the basin clean of waves and little fishes.
    The boy pushed by and moved aside a rag curtain,
    revealing a hollow filled with broken porcelain cups
    and chipped plates, random forks and spoons from
       mismatched sets,
    dolls with heads and dolls without. Their cubby looked
adored and alive, their well-used toys entwined with vines in
       the bushes.

The woman crouched and crawled on her knees after the
       children,
    her skirt and hair sweeping the dust, her long body
    compressing over and over like accordion folds,
    until she sat inside their fort, curled, tight and small
    as meat in a tree nut. She waited, eyes cast down,
    for one of them to speak. Instead they let the silence
    hang like the cups and dolls in the shrubs, waiting for use,
    and fixed instead small holes in the shelter, pinning back
the branches ripped free by the wind and making the roof less
       slack.

And then, without reserve they began to play as if
    they'd always kept a woman with a stitched mouth
    for playmate or prop within their secret forest hut.
    The girl brewed tea from air. She served it cold with cakes

made from clay lumps, dried and cracked, that came from
    the floor.
Her brother cut a wand to use as his hunting spear,
then left the females to hunt for boars in the field he called
the Great Wide Plain. Against the walls his shadow grew
and fell throughout the day, while the girl concocted a witch's
    brew.

And all the while the woman with the frog tongue
    sat beside the chattering girl and wove a bowl
    from reeds and grasses within arms reach. Her fingers rent
    and laced and fixed the whips as if she'd spent her life
    teasing useful shapes from stuff that wouldn't bend.
    The girl exclaimed and clapped her hands fast together
    when the woman tied the final knot and filled the bowl
    with spools, rocks, buttons, pennies and bottle caps—
        whatever
she found inside her pockets that gleamed and flashed in the
        light like treasure.

She knew she'd found a friend. Even the boy grinned
    when shown the bowl by his excited sister (but asked
    she make a basket large enough to hold his kill,
    the dragon he'd slain and dropped on the ground outside the
        hut).
    In answer, she raised her mute face up to the fading sun.
    She crawled toward the door, unfolding her stiff legs
    past the children, and into the early evening air.
    The children grumbled and claimed they didn't want to go.
So she started down the path, and it wasn't long before they
        followed.

Mama, Where are Their Parents?

For the first time, the woman with the frog tongue
is forced to consider a story other than her own.

At night she lays awake and wonders what makes these children
    walk
into the woods each day. (*Once a woman stabbed her finger while
    sewing,*

*then watched her blood drop and crawl through snow on the
    window sill.*
She gave birth to a daughter, and shortly after, she died.

*Once a woman craved a root that burned her mouth with its light-
    ning taste.*
*She made her husband steal it from a witch's garden. The witch stole
    her baby.*)

What mother doesn't listen with alarm while her daughter
    prattles on
about the lady in the woods, her silent, stitched mouth,

and her isolated tower? What father doesn't forbid these visits,
or his son accepting her weird gifts, fashioned from reeds and
    grasses?

(*Once a woman drank the mead a fairy brewed
from reptile parts. Her son was born a frog.*)

Who does or doesn't miss them when they do or don't come
    home?
She wonders why she never cared to wonder like this before.

(Once a woman fell asleep on a tuft of grass, and she conceived
a talking pig. Once a woman ate juniper berries until she bloated

from happiness. She gave birth to a daughter. And yes, she died.)
Who made the boy that worsted coat? Who tied the knots

on the girl's small shoes? Who shook the green pollen dust
each evening from their tangled hair? (*Once a girl swallowed a*
    rose leaf

and her girl's body swelled with a child. The fairies said she was just
    a girl
giving birth to a girl. No big deal.) And then, without an answer
    and before she sleeps,

she dwells for just a moment on the time she heard her father
    weep:
Her mother stood before him, unknowable and blind as rock.

Chapter VI: The Children Have a Request
(Mediation)

The season stretched itself thin, weakened by storms and heat.
    Inside the damp, shadowy space of the children's fort,
    the woman with the frog tongue wove baskets and bowls
    with tight, interlocked laces, while her silk stitches
    began to fray and lengthen. The gap between her lips
    widened to where the children could see the white of her
      teeth.
    They stared at her, sometimes; she saw them clench their
      jaws
    and try to speak to each other without moving their mouths.
Before long they'd begin to laugh, and she'd shake with relief at
      the sound.

Then one day, when the trees broke into glittering shards
    of gold and red and green, and light spun pinwheels above
    their heads as they walked together between the falling
      leaves,
    the girl looked at the woman and asked if she had a name.
    At this, the woman jerked to a stop. The old surge,
    the impulse to speak that rose within her belly and chest,
    overwhelmed. She wanted the girl and boy to know her
      name.
    Her tongue, rolled tightly and barred from moving inside its
      cage,
strained against her teeth and cheeks, contorting her face with
      its rage.

The boy stepped back when he saw the change on the
      woman's face.
    The girl moved closer, though, to pat the hand she held

like she might a frightened kitten or skittish, fallen bird.
Let's guess your name, she said. The woman's jaw fell slack,
as much as the stitches allowed. Her panic passed away.
The boy saw her relax and began to hop around.
A game, a game, he chanted. Across her eyes the sun
sliced its blade, and though her vision bled with its light,
she felt cheered by the girl's hand and the boy's excitement.

Aurora. Jezebel. Serafina, guessed the girl.
Her brother laughed and grabbed a fallen branch, whacking
the moss-covered roots of the trees surrounding them.
The woman laughed, too, short bursts of air through her
nose.
Her happiness shocked them all. The boy laughed again,
a raucous sound, and she looked the little girl in the eye.
A curve tested her mouth's seams, more grimace than grin,
but the girl smiled back and sighed with some relief. Then
she reached
toward the woman and pulled her close, until they were cheek
to cheek.

The girl's face, cold and smooth, smelled of the moss and earth
her brother lashed and whipped with vigor into the air.
The woman with the frog tongue hugged the girl loosely,
as if those little shoulder blades were planes of cloud,
a shifting mist she could see and feel between her arms
but couldn't collect, or hold, or keep for her very own.
The girl stepped back yet kept her hands by the woman's face.
Her small, thin fingers hovered before the fraying threads.
Why don't you take these out? she asked, as she touched each
ragged end.

At this the boy stopped his joyful assault of the trees
    and ran to see for himself what they discussed each night
    when walking home: her muffled, choked murmurings,
    the gray lattice unraveling across her mouth.
    He peered closely at each loose stitch, searching beyond
    her lips for whatever monster she'd locked so poorly inside.
    He found no monster, just a hint of pink tongue.
    So he shrugged, said *Yes*, and spun on his heel to resume his
        game.
The girl jumped up and down, shouting: *And then you'll tell us*
    your name!

The woman watched the boy whip tree roots free of moss,
    the tufts spinning into the air and separating,
    becoming dust, the dark green spores like beaks of birds
    that plummet toward the rocky earth without fear.
    She watched the girl's hair lift and fly away from her head,
    the wind dividing its strands, the way it hung, suspended
    like dust in the sun, then sank like spores: a sudden drop.
    She worked her mouth from side to side, and by degrees
opened her lips enough to burble a sound that said: *Maybe.*

Chapter VII: She Grows a Second Heart
(Struggle and Branding)

That night she woke to find another oddity:
    during sleep her heart had split or twinned itself,
    and where one muscle pumped before, now beat two.
    Her blood coursed through her veins twice as fast as before,
    and over those paths her skin buzzed and stammered, like
      wire
    strung tautly between two poles and charged with load.
    As if she'd run for miles across rolling hills,
    as if inside her chest two fists beat time all day,
beneath the bone she sped at death in the most alive way.

The day crawled while her two hearts raced. Above the fire
    she set a series of clocks to ticking. She watched the flames,
    sometimes leaning close enough to feel the heat
    singe her stitches a deeper shade, their fibers scorching
    until they curled, like dark froth spilling from her mouth.
    But when her hearts began to flicker more, and faster
    than she could stand, she turned her eyes to the clocks'
      marked faces
    and drew comfort from the second hands' neurotic twitch.
Every minute witnessed meant another minute lived.

Beneath her breastbone her strange second heart pulsed harder.
    She sensed the muscle, like her tongue, would leap and fly
    away from her body if her body let it go.
    She took the silver-handled knife and incised a cross
    above the cavity where her hearts ballooned together,
    jostling for room and dominance. The flaps of skin,
    pale as egg shell, trembled slightly. A head appeared.
    A bird with obsidian eyes emerged wet with her blood,
shook to shed its burden, and leapt toward the rafters above.

She watched the bird and felt air seep into the space
    it left behind, her single heart unrivaled but lonely
    in its great room. The wound bled slowly, healing fast
    to a pale silver scar, flaps falling back to close
    neatly over the bone, which laid itself again
    like lines of track or scaffolding across her chest.
    The bird flew to the window's sill, and ticked its head
    to look back at the woman. A slight breeze, cool and calm,
caressed its dark wings, and it leapt for the steady branch of
    that arm.

Chapter VIII: She Removes the Stitches
(Victory and Liquidation)

The fire in the hearth sparked and fumed. The clocks struck
    the hour in one long reprimand, their faces closed
    to further discussion. They ticked the seconds begrudgingly.
    The whole room seemed angry, as if each object mourned
    her loss of the little bird, its potential friendly noise
    and chaos, its brief disruption of stasis and constant gloom.
    Inside her mouth the frog tongue protested too, and pushed
    against her teeth and lips as it never had before,
attempting to stretch and unfold beyond her aching jaw.

She gave in. Her will collapsed like the tunnels dug by voles
    through her sad, neglected garden, and shadows jumped
    all around her, as if they knew her thoughts. She fumbled,
    searching between the clocks for the silver-handled knife,
    blind and out of breath with fear at her decision.
    She found it glinting on the floor, hot from the fire.
    It burned her fingertips and palm as she lifted the blade
    up to her mouth and nicked the weakest center stitch.
She pulled it slowly, thread through flesh, and her stomach
    turned and kicked.

The other stitches fell more easily, and soon
    her mouth was bare but for the holes the needle had made.
    Her bottom lip sank slowly and then her tongue unfurled.
    Instead of falling, loose and heavy as it had
    before in the goblin's shop, it uncurled and whipped the air.
    The line of clocks along the mantle smashed and hurtled
    against each other and then the floor, glass faces shattered.
    Each fragment sparkled with the fire's refracted light.
Her tongue recoiled, the muscle contracting and snapping back
    inside.

Suddenly, she felt the need to be away
from the fire's heat and searing light, the glittering,
fractured clocks, their mangled arms and splintered faces.
Down the stairs she fled and tripped, almost tumbling.
A need had spread through her bones and skin, an impulse
borne
with her unstitched mouth and muscular tongue, the power
she felt
from letting her body do what a body will always do
without restraint. Then into the forest's shadows she reeled,
through trees and patches of filmy moonlight, until she reached
the field.

The full moon lit the long grass with a stark gray sheen.
Above those slender stalks a constellation of moths
and lightning bugs hovered, minute stars changing their
shape
and story every minute, myth after myth
reborn and retold. The woman watched them, glad to breathe
the sharp, chill air so cold it burned her lungs and nose,
far from the tower and all its trappings, clutter and theft.
Then her tongue shot out. It caught and gathered what it
found,
a writhing mass of wings and spindle antennae, into her mouth.

She almost choked when she realized the crackling, folded
bodies—
these living things—were bottled now inside her throat.
The powdered fabric of their wings clung to its sides,
adhered like cut wet grass patterns the sides of a blade
that strikes it down. And still their thin legs whirred until

they shook loose and detached, abandoning one fight
and plunging into another. She mourned their deaths,
    ashamed.
Yet even as she knelt in the dirt, overcome with guilt,
her mouth unleashed her tongue again. It returned with mites
    and ticks.

A bat veered through the swath of sky above, and her tongue
    extended its sticky length to catch those wings and not
    the large white moth the bat pursued. Before she could fight
    this weird muscle and its strange new appetite,
    her tongue shot back between her teeth with the vermin
        tucked
    inside its fleshy rolls; then tossed it, small as a mouse
    and torn from light and sound, into the cavernous space
    beyond her mouth. And there for a moment it hung,
        suspended
by shock and disgust, until her throat convulsed, and the bat
        descended.

The woman with the frog tongue began to wail,
    a sound more fierce than any she'd made for months, or
        years.
    She meant to release a long, loud scream, or something like
    the shrill caw from a bird of prey before its kill, or
    the fierce, foreboding drone of a locust swarm—yet instead
    there came a deep rumbling, a sound that shook her frame.
    The call was ugly; like nothing she'd heard from any beast
    she'd come upon before. The grass shook. Animals fled.
Exhausted, she slumped across the field to the children's fort,
        and slept.

Chapter IX: The Children Find Her Sleeping
(Return and Unrecognized Arrival)

On waking, she found a pair of small hands cupped her cheeks.
   The little girl's face had replaced the moon, and her brother
   orbited, making small, impatient sighs and grunts
  as he tried to find, in that cramped space, a better view.
   The girl moved her hands from the woman's cheeks and ran
   a finger softly along the pocks that scarred her lips.
   Then pressing gently, she scraped her nail along the flesh
   as if the threads were buried there, as if her skin
had overgrown the stitches, and now she kept them, too, within.

The threads, they're gone, she told her brother. He gave a nod.
   He looked relieved he didn't need to touch the scars,
   or venture closer. He stayed behind his sister's shoulder.
   The woman raised her aching head from the creek floor,
   her throat dry with its dust, and her sticky tongue curled
   like larvae inside her mouth's cocoon. For now, it slept.
   Why were you sleeping here? What happened to your lips?
   they asked at once, like baby birds clamoring for worms.
Her answer rose with bile in her throat. She choked it back; it
     burned.

The woman motioned to the door of the little hut.
   Beyond the entrance, the clouds were sketched with streaks
     of coal.
   Reluctantly, the children crawled outside and stood
   to wait for her in the fog. Their cheeks and foreheads
     glistened
   with drops of mist, as if tears streamed down their solemn
     faces.
   She raised herself from the ground and shook her skirt free
   of dirt and lichen, grateful to breathe in the cool, damp air.

She savored its balm along her throat; that muscle felt bruised
and scored by the bat's sharp claws and spiny wings. It ached
    with rebuke.

She turned and stared into the children's expectant faces.
    Her lips eased open slowly; a smile through locked teeth hid
    her tongue from view. The girl smiled back, a mirrored grin,
    and even her brother relaxed. He turned to kick at stones.
    His small feet stirred the creek bed's dust to shoot up
    in a brown cloud, and gravel vaulted over the edge.
    A bird hidden inside a tangle of weeds shot out,
    its dark head arrowed toward unoccupied sky, and then:
the frog tongue snapped, recoiled, and the bird hung from her
    mouth, dead.

The girl's expression began to change. Her smile blurred,
    losing its arc, and her cheeks and jaw and brow grew hard,
    jutting from under her skin. She aged in the rapid beat
    and sudden, cruel cessation of the bird's wings.
    Her brother whipped around, confused, unsure he could trust
    his sight in those seconds, or what he saw right now in these:
    The woman, red-faced and fumbling, extracted the bird
    adhered to her tongue—so small, but an awkward fit for her
    mouth.
Then his face contorted, too. He pulled on his sister's arm,
    shouting:

Let's go, get out, let's go, but the girl couldn't make out
    his words; she heard only a howl, the sound of grief.
    She thought it might be the bird, its body broken but living;
    but the woman cried, the woman wailed as feathers fell

from broken wings that spread lifeless across her hand.
That sound, the woman's grief, finally reached the girl.
As if she wouldn't hear what she couldn't see, she turned
to run across the field, pulling her brother along,
and scattering groups of sparrows until the field was empty
of song.

Mama, Couldn't She Eat a Fly? Because
  She Has a Frog Tongue

The woman doesn't want to eat the bird, or the moth,
or swath her tongue in gnats or fruit flies.

Her tongue will not bend the way her mind dictates, in the way
her arm, sometimes late at night, abdicates the bed's realm

and travels through the forest on its own. She feels a kind of
    static
where it used to lie, like a cloud of bees buzzing at her
    shoulder.

She dreams that her dismembered arm, a white branch stark
against the dark oak leaves, swings between the trees

and then crawls on its fingertips along the ground.
Her nail beds fill with black, wet earth. Her forearm glows

with the nighttime's condensation: a slick, pale ember
in the moon's occasional light. Beams push through the forest
    canopy,

highlight the crook of her elbow bent above a spider's lattice,
or hooked around a clump of brush. Her arm, absent from
    sleep,

has great adventures. And then she wakes and shifts her weight,
only to discover something cold and clammy in the sheets
    beside her,

a lump of flesh she cannot call her own. Her other arm,
the one remaining in her bed, loyal until the end,

investigates by lifting the offending, foreign object
and then, in shock, dropping it.It slaps against the mattress

and then the pain begins, the necessary hurt that comes
with reattachment. The cloud of bees lengthens and attacks,

a hundred stingers lodged inside her skin, and dissipates
like fog obscured by burning sun. And then she is aware

that her arm was always there, by her side,
and neither part, arm or mind, is happy when she awakes.

Chapter X: How Will This Story End?
X.i. Lightning
(Transfiguration and Punishment)

I.

Once the children left the meadow, their ghosts hanging
    like clouds of dust and fog that couldn't burn away
    in the wet air, the woman's panic thickened, too,
    as if it were layers of sky descended, blanketing
    her skin and stopping her mouth and nose until breathing
    became a chore, a ragged labor, and then it crawled
    to fits and starts, full stops followed by deep inhalations.
    The sparrow's carcass slid from her open palm to the ground.
When the dust began to crawl with ants, she staggered back to
    her tower.

The hearth was filled with glowing ash, its smoldering light
    the only moving part of the room. Inside her chamber
    the air was slick with cold and dew, its surfaces
    collecting water beads and the sheen of saturation.
    The knife she'd used to free her heart, that distressed bird,
    lay among the cogs and wheels from the shattered clocks,
    the fine blade dull with blood. She picked it up, and pain,
    its phantom, flashed inside her chest like sudden applause.
She opened her mouth and raised the knife. Then she cut her
    tongue off.

Her mouth, hot with its fresh wound, filled with dark liquid.
    Its overflow spilled to the floor, a wash that pooled and
      gleamed
    more red in the weak light of the room. She threw her tongue,
    uncurled and limp, onto the ash and piled wood
    on top, hiding its monstrous length. She lit the tinder.

Slow as sunrise, flames began to rise. Light broke
across the marble floor and onto the woman's face.
She thrust the knife into the blaze so it burned clean;
then she raised its blade to the stump and seared the flesh. Her
wound was sealed.

She found again the silk, and the needle made of stone,
and through the open pocks along her lips she sewed
again the stitches, even though her mouth was emptied
of all threat. Blood that smeared her teeth clung to the
threads,
staining them pink. The face she saw in the mirror looked
like she'd been painted wrong: a blur instead of a mouth,
her pupils lost within their dark brown irises,
her hair matted with dust and laced with twigs. At length,
she cleaned the tower floor, and then herself, and then she slept.

After fitful dreams she rose to a fitful world.
She watched the sun regain the sky, its cold gray light
tearing the shadowy trees to ribbons, whips of branches
that lashed back, raking clouds, refusing the sky its tether.
Something pulled at her as well. Small spheres of tangled
leaves tumbled across the brittle, brown lawn
and broke apart in the woods, catching in brambles that
shook
as if they feared being crushed by the world overhead,
but she ignored the warning. Down the tower steps she fled

and into the building storm, its argument loud in her ears,
its anger deafening, its sudden, vain tears
washing her face as she walked between the trees and brush.

The field, where just the day before she'd scared the children,
   moved its many hands in protest, the grass bent
   away from her footsteps, every blade loathing her touch.
   Against the wind she walked, pushed back by its solid arm,
   while thunder shook the air and lightning pared the sky.
A white bolt needled through her body into the ground, and she
      died.

II.

Two seasons passed. When the children began to feel safe,
   emboldened by sunshine, green leaves budding and birds
      returned,
   they found her remains: a batch of bones regurgitated
   by some monstrous owl, or dragon, a mess they barely knew
   as human, let alone belonging to *her*, the woman who'd once
   woven them gifts and kept them company in silence.
   Her dress was just a rag melted into the earth.
   The boy kicked loose a bone from the overgrown grass that
      choked
with her debris, and he held it aloft, as if he'd conquered a foe.

His sister remained more solemn, frightened by the ants
   that streamed in long black tears from the skull's empty stare,
   its teeth forever locked in the same disturbing smile.
   While her brother vanquished monsters with his femur-sword,
   she hurried back and forth between the creek and the bones,
   shuttling cups and saucers full of earth and rocks
   to cover the skull's unbearable grin. The little grave
   rose above the grass, a marker and reminder—
but they forgot about her, as children do, over time.

X.ii. Love
(Transfiguration and Wedding)

Once the children left the meadow, their ghosts hanging
    like clouds of dust and fog that couldn't burn away
    in the wet air, the woman's panic thickened, too,
    as if it were layers of sky descended, blanketing
    her skin and stopping her mouth and nose until breathing
    became a chore, a ragged labor, and then it crawled
    to fits and starts, full stops followed by deep inhalations.
    The sparrow's carcass slid from her palm to the ground. She
      bored
the bird a narrow grave in the dirt, then staggered into the forest.

She wandered for many days, her tongue lashing out
    at random, moving things: twigs falling, darting birds,
    whatever remained as winter began to shoulder its yoke
    and rake the forest floor with cold, unforgiving air.
    Sometimes she ate what she caught, and sometimes she
      wrestled guilt
    until it won, and then she'd scrape the wings or scraps
    of leg or skull from off her tongue, and spend the night
    curled around her belly's empty bowl, amazed
and stunned by her hunger: its swift return, its pangs fierce and
    abrupt.

Her hunger kept her moving, too. Her sore belly
    and aching throat propelled her onward. Afraid her body
    would grow some new strange part if she stopped to rest for
      long,
    she moved through the thinning trees and low brush swiftly,
      until
    a road appeared under her feet, and she chose to walk
    along its smooth, bare path instead of stumbling through
      leaves.

And yet, as if her legs missed resistance, the weight
   of wet blades, fronds, and needles that clung with every step,
she felt exhausted, as if their hindrance had spurred her early
      strength.

At last she reached a house, a blacksmith's shop that squatted
   low by the road. She heard the saturated toll
   of metal stretched and shaped, the hammer's repeating arc
   forging holes where holes had never been before.
   She attended to every clang, the old familiar surge
   rising within her chest. With every peal her tongue
   twitched behind her teeth, syllables waiting to launch
   but coiled inside the muscle. She walked to the open door,
and watched the metal change and adapt a soft, more supple
      form.

As the blacksmith banged the wrought iron he felt her gaze
   searing his back, less bearable than the forge's heat
   that charred the metal black and made it bend like clay.
   He bore the heat of both the forge and her eyes until
   the last note wrung from his hammer and chisel hung like
      smoke
   along the air. He coughed to clear his lungs and turned,
   then jumped, expecting a patron and not this woman who
      stared,
   half-starved and threadbare. He raised his hand, wordless,
      and gestured
to a chair. She nodded back and entered, each step slow and
      measured.

He stood in silence, expecting she would speak. She shifted
   in her seat. The fire cast half her face in light

while shadow blacked the other half, a frown misshaping
her brow and cheeks, her tongue like ore inside her mouth.
Before long it would leap without her leave, and tell
this man a story that he'd believe whether or not
the story belonged to her, and so she opened her lips.
Her fingers rolled the muscle out for him to see,
its pink length stretched out fully, her fingers trembling with
    fatigue.

He frowned a little, but didn't move away in shock,
   or grow pale with disgust, as she expected. Instead,
   he bent his head closer, and narrowed his dark eyes.
   She was, he said, *an odd bird caught in a rare net.*
   Her heart opened and closed its small wings, preened at this:
   the first strain of sympathy she'd heard in many years;
   his lack of fear; that he stayed despite the oddity
   she bared to him, this weird, tensile flag of surrender.
A plea brimmed her eyes, and she slowed her ragged breath
    with effort.

He moved closer, his large hand raised to touch her tongue,
   which stretched like a tether, taut and red, away from her jaw
   and curled its end around her thumb like a bird's claw
   or possum tail. Then it sensed the change in the air and
    snapped
   back into her mouth. He nodded and stood, his shadow
   falling across her face. *Why enter here*, he asked,
   if you won't let me do what I could do to help?
   She knew his words were true. The look in his eyes made
    sense.

She opened her mouth again. He drew a pair of tongs from the
     bench,

     and stretched her tongue until it spanned the space between
          them.
     Then quick and deft as a surgeon he clipped the organ with
          shears
     just behind her teeth. The bulk of the muscle fell
     heavy and limp to the floor. Then he soldered shut the wound:
     his tongs a lathe, turning the flesh and forging a point
     from the blunt cut, a fine, clean end she could use to speak.
     When he was done, her tongue burned darkly within her
          mouth.
     He poured a cup of water. She drank, and steam spilled
into the air, diluting the iron musk of blood that lingered.

Her mouth lukewarm like dampened coal, the woman bent
     and moved her severed tongue from where it lay on the floor.
     She flung it into the fire and watched it curl like leaves
     between the coals. Then the smithy closed the doors of the
          forge
     and led her up some stairs to a small room, where he made
     a straw pallet beside his bed, and said she could rest
     here if rest was what she wanted. So she spent
     some nights on the pallet, and days learning his trade, until
he taught her how to be his wife, his helpmeet. They found she
          was skilled.

No longer the woman with the frog tongue, but a wife
     and soon a mother, the woman lived a calmer life,

one fraught with common tensions and ordinary problems,
the kind conjured by home and husband—not the stuff
of fairy tales—and yet these small trials made her happy.
Her tongue healed well, though not completely. Just enough
for her to speak essential words like *yes*, like *love*.
  She practiced them over her infant girl, who cried back
in trills and chirps, a voice honest and wholly unabashed.

X.iii. Livestock
(Transfiguration)

Once the children left the meadow, their ghosts hanging
    like the dust clouds and fog that couldn't burn away
    in the wet air, the woman's panic thickened, too,
    as if it were layers of sky descended, blanketing
    her skin and stopping her mouth and nose until breathing
    became a chore, a ragged labor, and finally crawled
    to fits and starts. Then, suddenly, she stopped fighting
    her nature. She shoved the bird back in her mouth and
      chewed
what she could manage, the air filling with down and bone
      spewed

from the awkward dance of maw and teeth and giant tongue.
    To eat like this was work, but oddly satisfying.
    She looked back at the fort, then across the field where silence
    grew like mist; and the children's terror was also there,
    static preceding a storm. She knew she couldn't stay.
    She reached inside the hut and grabbed what her fingers
      touched
    first, a small doll's head and a mangled pair of forks.
    She shoved them into her skirt's pockets, then staggered away
into the woods, exhausted, where she wandered for many days.

Eventually, she found again the hobgoblin's shop:
    a line of thick smoke rose from the crumbling chimney stack,
    as if a massive fire raged inside the home.
    She knocked, her knuckles burning from the wood's heat,
    but when the door swung open the room inside was clear,
    cool, and clean. In the dark shadows she saw his form
    seated, at ease, as if he waited for her to appear.
    Show me, he urged. She cleared her throat, then let her tongue
whip the air, so he might see the monster that she'd become.

He chuckled, a low rumble that shook the ground and walls.
   Are you still unhappy? he asked. She found she didn't know
   the answer, despite her swollen throat, her tired feet,
   her lonely heart, and scars that pocked her once smooth skin.
   Unhappiness was not the language she would choose.
   Weary, perhaps, would be the better word; or *dry*—
   she felt brittle as leaves blanched by the winter sun.
   Also, *confused*—for all she'd lived, so little she knew
about the world outside herself, other than its rebuke.

She raised her hands in the air like two cupped sides of a scale,
   unsure of how to tip them, unsure of what they held.
   In one, the hobgoblin placed a root shaped like a man.
   Her hand bobbed under its weight, a cloud of earth sinking
   through her fingers down to her feet. Its dense, cool bulk
   recalled her garden, those early days, and the children's fort,
   where, sat in dust, she wove them countless toys with grass.
   And in the other hand he placed a living bird:
Her voice, her metamorphic heart, and her appetite converged.

The bird ruffled its wings and settled into her hand.
   Inside her mouth her tongue pulsed, but she bit down hard
   and turned her head toward the room while her hand released
   its catch. The bird leapt for the light beyond the door,
   the sudden, frantic beating of its wings a fracture
   in the room's stillness. Dust and down spiraled above
   her outstretched hand and then drifted slowly to the floor.
   She turned back to the small, gnarled man, whose eyes
      agreed
with her choice. He bade her sit while he steeped the mandrake
      into tea.

The tea smelled fecund and loamy, rich and warm with decay:
    like maple leaves and cut grass dampened, left to slump
    and soften over months. With her tongue pinned back,
      unrolled
    below her chin, she threw the draught down her throat.
    The liquid's heat wormed through her, warming her gut
      and skin
    until she felt she'd caught fire. The shadows moved
    along the walls, contorting, a dark mural that changed
    again and again and pantomimed her entire life.
She grew dizzy watching its circus act. She closed her eyes,

and knew that she was changing, too, like the shadows had,
    some of her parts lengthening, others collapsing down,
    pulled toward the floorboards. Her center grew closer
    to earth than she'd ever been before. Some parts became
    calcified, rockier, while others turned more soft,
    bone and cartilage exchanged for pliant fat
    and flexing muscle. Her insides stormed with bolts of pain.
    And then it stopped. A sudden peace invaded, ceased
the riot of flesh and vertebrae. She'd changed into a beast.

The hobgoblin took some rope and tied a lead to her neck.
    He pulled it tight and walked her back into the forest,
    her four feet leaving small triangular dents in the ground,
    her broad nose snuffling through winter's detritus and frost
    that rimed the roots of trees. She did what her body told her,
    her mind quiet inside its new shell like a cat
    curled in a window, content to watch the world enact
    its pageantry from a distance. The goblin walked her through
the woods to a pasture. He cut her lead and left her there
    among ewes

and heifers and others of her kind, a sisterhood
   that milled about the green and ate and slept and acted
   only when they were acted upon. So husbandry goes.
   The farmer who found her wondered, confused, if he'd been
      wrong
   about his livestock, numbers, the creatures he herded for
      days
   between the barn and these rolling hills, but then
      dismissed
   his worry, as men do, when faced with greater concerns.
   So there she stayed and thrived, accepted as never before
while birthing sons and daughters, each a coda to her story.

3. Minor Gods

A Woman

But before the three gods could begin to create,
they had to get rid of the frost giant, Ymir.

I.

Each morning the sunrise runs its rough wet tongue
along the earth and, over time, strips salt from its rock.

The shape of my life emerges: Here, an outcrop of hip.
There, my breast—a precipice from which my children,
also rock, will detach and like a landslide, fall.

These shifting sands are anxiety. This strata, fear.
And underneath, there flows a stirring, liquefied heat.

The creature who wakes and clambers inch by inch away
from this bed of slag is born fighting a great hunger.
It threatens her, like water after rain consumes
the dunes and tender grasses exposed along the shore.

II.

By sunset, I am a creature sucking greedily
on the last light of day. I eat and eat, and yet

I am always hungry, and my children are always hungry.
We fight for what we want. We grow beyond our needs.

III.

Somewhere in this mire, my better self gives birth
to better children, embodiments of faith and love,
not frost and rock and teeth that never stop their gnashing.

May those better children find me and destroy
the wild monster I have become. May they take my body,
my blood and brine, to build the world they'll someday rule.

My brains and skull for sky. My hair for forests of ash
and alder; my flesh for moss beneath the leaves and clouds.

May this hunger be put to rest. May I return
to sediment, the dregs from which I took my birth.

A Woman, Split

As long as the ash tree stood, the world of the Aesir would last,
for it was Yggdrasil, the world tree.

I.

Imagine I am a tree.
And at my roots I hold
three selves, three sisters, stacked.

One squats and bears the weight
of the other two combined
and balanced on her back.

Her spine like ironwood
remains unmoved, despite
the ways her sisters shift.

The middle one distrusts
the girl on whom she rests
but shrugs to free herself

from the legs around *her* neck.
She seethes with jealousy
and bites her sister's knees.

The third cannot bite back.
She hunches low and frets
about the roots, which grow

in knots above her head.
Beneath this canopy
their shadows tremble and blend.

II.

Now imagine I am three.
Not the tree. Instead,
a totem made of flesh

beneath a wooden sky:
my many fingers spin
the thread of possible lives.

Gray cord denotes a life
colored dun, a hue
with toil in every fiber.

To ride this line means work,
and only work, and strife,
and weariness, and death.

The second kind of thread
gleams bright as foam on waves
convulsing after storms:

This for a woman filled
with joy and anguish because
she loves, and then love fails.

The third, the gold, the best
is saved for a woman bold,
a saintly heroine,

who guides herself through toil
and love without the scars
amassed through tribulation.

III.

Imagine this is me:
A woman split, like lightning
forks a sapling oak

and each tine grows toward
the light it needs to live
after birth's first flash.

Can such a woman be
content with just one fate
between her squabbling selves?

Won't they start to knot
and cut the threads they spin
when envy cramps their hands?

Won't they come to yearn
for lives apart despite
their fear of solitude?

Together they make a wheel.
Like spindles, their fingers twist
ethereal batt to yarn.

Lives, like handspun, pool
around the ancient tree.
Yet no matter how they long

to occupy the lives
they spin, they won't unravel
from one another yet.

Conjoined by fate, each girl
is just a cog that moves,
a piece of a spinning wheel.

A Woman, Tempted

*But still they had to pass through dangerous and
bewitched waters.*

I.

I lash myself to the mast. The siren sings
and I would hear his light and sinewy notes.

The knot is meant to restrain. I need the knot
because it keeps me safe. The air may shift
between the coils wrapped around me, but
the hitch is complex. It tightens when I move.

My faithless hands deny this undertaking.
They chafe the rope, and the knot frays, but holds.

II.

We pass the island where dead women lie
open-mouthed, as if struck mid-aria.

Around them stretch the bodies of their children,
small, stiff arms and legs arranged at their sides
as if they were planks of wood to walk across.

By them we know the measure and the cost
of the siren's exquisite song. The husbands' entrails
loop the shore like seaweed in red foam.

III.

O my husband, you are both seducer
and faithful spouse, the one who urges me
to danger, and then waits for me at home.

You know the risk and yet you chant and praise
until I think I cannot fail this course
I steer toward.The siren's melody
is just as brash and full of adulation.
You and he are brothers in this art.

IV.

I cannot trust that I will pass this test.
I hear his song and parts of me respond.

He sings of lands I lived in long ago.
He sings a language I thought I had forgotten.
He reminds me of past glories, like stars
I used to follow when skies were dark and clear.

That voice would ravish me; like splintered teeth
each note and word delivered by that note
tear wounds that will not close. They are that deep.

I want to lay my body down and bleed
among the calcified remains—no thought
for what and who and why it all will end.

V.

But then the seas change and I drift away,
far from the operatic voice that churned
the smaller sea within me. The drama ends.
The ropes go slack and I can move about.

Most days, I float unfettered in the ocean,
buoyed by silken waves that lap my skin
because there is no ship or boat or voice.

You float there, too—our bodies side by side,
like driftwood loosed on changeable water.

A Woman, Culpable

One day as Hera looked down on earth, she spied a small
dark thundercloud where no cloud should have been.

Perhaps this other man—the one whose song
felt familiar as my own heart's strain—
maybe he *was* birthed from his father's thigh,
then raised and spoiled by half-clad women;
or born misshapen by his father's mischief,
horned and cleft of foot because his mother
resisted—but not enough—his father's love.

It would be easier to see the man
as not a man—but satyr, monster, god
or godlike fiend—and not the man he is,
a mortal who plays the character he writes
as he acts, masked and costumed with desire.

Do not blame the one who performs so well—
his job was to convince. So he came to me
dressed as someone else—I came to him
soft and unnatural, a beast from another myth:
white as froth and lovely with deception,
compelled and bearing the yoke of what she covets.

A Woman, Struggling

Hope gave him back his songs, and, playing and singing,
he walked down the dark, steep path.

I.

When we met the world was gray and dead and full of ice.
No—we met before that day, sometime in spring.
Revise.
There was an older, previous season, absent
of any errant spark that could light the wrong fire
when we shook hands. A fire didn't need to be lit.
We warmed ourselves with different bodies, back then.

II.

This story is so complicated. Confused,
and without direction. It doesn't know what it wants to be.
It begins with a man and a wife, and another: that old song.
One chases, one flees, one takes a journey to hell and back
(or maybe all of them do), and it proves difficult
to tell which role is played by whom. This is not a success,
this play. What audience stays to witness such a disaster?

III.

Forgive this silence strung loosely between us:
the contrary chord it plays is loud enough
to insult your well-trained ear. I keep it slack
because I must; I am learning to check my impulsive bent

for making noise and forcing sound where sound has begged
a rest, for release a measure or more. I tried to suspend
the closing notes we played. I'd hoped they'd satisfy.

IV.

I could not look back. (That rule existed before
the journey began—we can't pretend it wasn't there.)
I couldn't charm my way and my marriage out of this one.
To turn my head and break a rule, however odd,
would be to lose the very thing for which I'd risked
the dark and torment. And I knew what lay beyond
the wall of light ahead—my own guilt, like a mob
drunk and bitter, waiting to tear me limb from limb.

A Woman, Addressing Doubt

"The father is bad, the mother is worse," said Odin in disgust.
"No good can ever come from the offspring of such parents."

I.

If *you* are the god of mischief, and I'm the angry ogress, your
    giant wife,
how do we navigate the litter of bone and muscle we create,
torn from the mortals we've consumed, the people we
    beguiled to sate
our own weird appetites? Their carcasses lay shredded, beyond
    revival.

Or are these strips not strips of flesh but fabric, ripped from our
    victims' clothes?
And the blood that's spilled, just the blood that stains, and noth-
    ing more than a wash of red,
 nothing a pumping heart would miss? Look: though scratched,
    they still walk the earth.

Perhaps we are not as lethal or as fierce as we imagined ourselves—
deadly as poetry, and only when the listener allows the wound,
asks for it, baring his heart, exposing all his weakest parts for
    the kill.

II.

What a family we make: the lives that we've created, the multiples
housed in us both!The shapes we've assumed throughout the
    years hang like shadow
behind us, strange halos befitting the parents of such a mon-
    strous brood.

And what luck can they have, with such an ugly mother, with
   such a trickster dad?
How *can* I tell them they aren't bad, when I cast my face to water
and catch, in the light of the shallows, no plain of cheek that's
   fixed by time,
but instead a mask as gray and yielding as clay before the fire's
   heat?

How I shift! And how can I ignore or condemn your own shifting?
How can I not love our children, accursed with fangs and tails
   and flaws
beyond description? How can I not adore the way you play with
   them?

III.

If we may be redeemed, let it be for the way you hold our
   daughter's hand
when we come to judgment. Let it be for my other shape, your
   other wife,
who holds the cup above your face to keep the venom from
   eating your eyes.

Who else would do this task until the end: when the world
   collapses
on itself, the world our fathers and mothers built from a giant,
   fallen god,
and that our children will destroy for us out of loyalty, and love?

A Woman, Wrong

To gain greater power, he hanged himself on Yggdrasil's
wind-swept branches, Odin sacrificed to Odin.

I.

My father's shadow blurs the ground.
Above my head his feet, like tongues
inside brass bells, toll large, long notes
against the sunset's rigid walls.

Their sound proclaims the loss he's made.
But he hangs wrong—just watch the branch
bend to excuse his weight, the kill
it shrugs from its complicit arms.

No sacrifice should be so final.
Something should remain: a breath.
A quickening. A seed beneath
the earth ready to sprout again.

II.

My mother hangs more fair—at least
she fights the cord. It pulls her skin
to white, a sunburst dividing blood
between horizons. Her body bucks,

an act more terrible than sound.
But this, too, is a failed blessing.
She would give her children everything
but this refusal to rest denies

the sacrifice its full meaning.
Gravity should win: in her limbs
a loosening, a sudden slackness,
despite the upturned faces below.

III.

I climb the tree determined to hang
the way that's right. I tie the knot
around my neck and drop my body
into the air that welcomes me.

I give myself to myself, and suffer
without speaking: eyes spread wide
as leaves newly unfurled, searching
for wisdom in shadows scattered below.

On the ninth day my eyes form shapes
from broken twigs along the ground.
They are the words that I would share,
the reason for this half-strung life.

But my children, little birds at play,
won't attend to the raspy sounds
I shout at them from up above.
They pick and toss the runes apart.

A Woman, Reflecting

He looked, instead, into Athena's polished shield, and shuddered at
the sight he saw mirrored there.

I.

I stare at my image: tiny black mouths
with fevered tongues unfold from the coils of my hair,
testing the air and the mirror's cold surface.

Each serpent's head rears at the sight
of its own ferocity, and my eyes petrify
from this honest glance—its magnitude and its might.

II.

But that's not it. It's not mine, that story,
or how a body reacts to its terror and loss.

In the myth, one of many versions, a woman
is made a monster for being raped; she is raped
for being playful, pliant, and meek; and then

she is slain, beheaded for her rage, punished
for bitterness. From her severed neck springs
a winged horse, and a man, his phallus deadly
and golden beside the blood from which he emerges.

III.

In this version of my life, I am not raped
by a careless god or spurned by a vengeful goddess.

I pose no danger to anyone, least of all
to me. Instead, I stand before the mirror,
stone-faced, listening for the sword's whistle,
willing its swift cut, and wishing to give birth.

Whatever comes, I want it to mean something,
like a severed head hung from a hero's shield.

A Woman, Responsible

*There, in his dark corner, he went on withering and shriveling till
at last he turned into a grasshopper, chirping for all eternity.*

Even the dawn forgets, or fails, to think
through a wish, to imagine the end that lies
beyond a wish's sweet beginnings: its flush,
its youth, its tender promise, the way it looks
at you, haloed in soft first light, and swears
that all your mornings will be fruitful, like this.

Because she is the dawn, she cannot curse
her own naïveté when she wakes and hears
the plaintive song her love sings in the dark,
his wizened face shaded by stalks of grass.

Because she is the dawn, she's wise and knows
regret has little use, cannot undo
the work her wish has wrecked upon her love,
that she must see her love made small and stooped,
taunted by a death that never comes.

Because she is the dawn, she accepts she made
a choice when she wished, and now her love is changed,
and when she wakes and lifts the night away
like bed sheets from the earth, she sees that change
anew but knows her shock will fade like stars.

What can she gain from sinking back with grief?
Her love grows old, but he sings his song for her.

A Man and Woman, Repairing

*The Deucalion race, made from stone, was hardier than the one
made from clay. The new mortals withstood better the stings of
Pandora's miseries . . .*

I.

After flood and fire, misfortunes imagined
and those too real, we are left with loneliness.

We walk along the wet or scorched earth,
the suck of mud or scuff of ash the sounds
our feet exchange. Our mouths are done with speech,
empty as dead volcanoes; nothing to say
but *O*, again and again, wet rings of fog
we breathe toward the sky. We cannot bear
to look down and see what we have done.

We brim with less desire now. We do not want
to know the cost of curiosity.

Our hope rattles inside its clay jar.

II.

Let misfortune buzz around our heads
like flies that circle and feed upon the dead.

Our loose coin, hope corralled, will pay our debts.
Its small voice chimes: *Rebuild. Rebuild. Rebuild.*

III.

So we throw the bones of our old lives,
for luck, in arcs over our shoulders: A score
of men appear behind your back—as many
women fall like shadow beyond my own.

They are our better selves, though not immune
from miseries. Instead, they bear the stings
of lust and greed and vanity like stones
withstand the heat from flames, or weather rain's
incessant beat for days and nights on end.
We see the grace our new lives wield and know
they will survive. An end is not disaster,
nor catastrophes an end. We lift
our hands toward the sky. A shrug or prayer,
the gesture speaks the same word: surrender.

She says, *Mama, I feel two beats on each side of me, so I think I have two hearts.* I answer, *When I was a little girl I read about the earth and the way it spins. Then at night when I lay in bed beside the big window in my room, and the crickets and cicadas sung to me through the dark while the scent of honeysuckle crawled past the window's sash, I'd have moments where I felt myself spun too, whirling very fast, as if I'd returned to that playground ride where the older kids kept running the carousel faster and faster, and eventually I whipped into the air, a little flag of blonde hair and corduroy snapping to and fro, my scream lost in the wind. I thought I was going to die. I'd recall that chaos, that lost control, later when I'd been tucked into my sheet and my hair smoothed and my mother sang goodnight. When she left the room I became the axis on which the world spun, whirling with it and growing dizzy from insect song and the scent of flowers opening in the humid dark. It is amazing what the mind draws forth.* I tell her, *I like your two hearts. I imagine they are birds, though I will tell you about your blood and the way it carries a word, repeated, through the pathways of your body. I want you to believe me. And yet, I want for you those summer nights, too, when you lie awake and imagine all the ways you don't.*

NOTES

The Woman with the Frog Tongue

The chapter subtitles of this long poem are taken from
Vlamidir Propp's "Thirty-One Functions [of the Fairy Tale],"
found in *Morphology of the Folktale,* translated by Laurence
Scott and published by University of Texas Press. Part of
Morphology is excerpted at the end of *The Classic Fairy Tales,*
an anthology of texts and criticism edited by Maria Tatar and
published by W. W. Norton and Company (1999).

The form of the poem borrows from Edmund Spenser's
"The Faerie Queene."

Minor Gods

In the spring and summer of 2011, my daughter and I read
two books by Ingri and Edgar Parin D'Aulaire: *D'Aulaires'
Book of Norse Myths,* published by the New York Review Chil-
dren's Collection (2005) and *D'Aulaires Book of Greek Myths,*
published by Delacorte, an imprint of Random House Chil-
dren's Books (2003). The section's title comes from *Greek
Myths* (page 70). The epigraphs for the poems come from the
text of both books, and some of the poems' images are pulled
from the books' illustrations.

"A Woman": The epigraph comes from "The First Gods and
Giants" (page 13) in *Norse Myths.* The three first Aesir gods
destroyed their *jotun* (giant) kinsman and used his body to
create the earth.

"A Woman, Split": The epigraph comes from "Yggdrasil, the World Tree" (page 31) in *Norse Myths* and the image of the three Norns, or "Fays of Destiny," stacked on each other's shoulders comes from the image on the chapter's first page.

"A Woman, Tempted": The epigraph comes from "The Golden Fleece" in *Greek Myths* (page 172) which tells the tale of Jason and the Argonauts, although the imagery in the poem is derived from Homer's *Odyssey*.

"A Woman, Culpable": The epigraph comes from "Hera" in *Greek Myths* (page 24), but the poem uses imagery from and refers to the stories of Zeus and Io, Zeus and Semele, the birth of Dionysus, and Pan.

"A Woman, Struggling": The epigraph comes from the section titled "Minor Gods, Nymphs, Satyrs and Centaurs" in *Greek Myths* and the tale of Orpheus (page 102).

"A Woman, Addressing Doubt": The epigraph comes from "Loki's Monstrous Brood" in *Norse Myths* (page 50). The god of mischief, Loki, takes an ogress wife with whom he has off-spring: a serpent, a hag, and a wolf. Odin exiles the children instead of killing them. Then, after causing the death of the beloved god Balder, Loki is condemned to everlasting torture. He is relieved of some of the torment by his other wife, Sigunn. Soon the rift between the jotuns and the gods escalates and results in the destruction of the world. Loki's children, Fenris, Hel, and Midgard's Serpent, do most of the damage.

"A Woman, Wrong": The epigraph comes from "Yggdrasil,
The World Tree" in *Norse Myths* (page 33). Odin hangs himself
and discovers runic letters, which makes him the wisest god,
or All-Father. He shares his knowledge with man, and thus
reading and writing exists on earth.

"A Woman, Reflective": The epigraph comes from the section
"Mortal Descendents of Zeus," and the tale of "Danaüs, Per-
seus, and the Gorgon," in *Greek Myths* (page 118), although
the imagery comes from multiple versions of the death of
Medusa. (The D'Aulaire text refers only to the birth of Pega-
sus, and omits the simultaneous birth of Chrysaor.)

"A Woman, Responsible": The epigraph comes from the
section "Minor Gods, Nymphs, Satyrs and Centaurs" in *Greek
Myths* (page 81) and the tale of Eos, the dawn, and her love for
the mortal Tithonus. Eos asks Zeus to grant Tithonus eternal
life but neglects to ask that he be given eternal youth as well.

"A Man and Woman, Repairing": The epigraph comes from
the section "Minor Gods, Nymphs, Satyrs and Centaurs" in
Greek Myths (page 77) and the tale of Deucalion and Pyrrha,
who survived a flood that Zeus sent to wipe out the human
race after they were infected with the miseries from Pando-
ra's jar. Zeus felt pity for the two survivors and instructed
them to create a new race of humans made from stones they
tossed over their shoulders.

ACKNOWLEDGMENTS

My deep, sincere gratitude to the editors of the following publications for printing my poems. They are reprinted here by permission.

The first section (titled here "The Sow") was published as a chapbook by Hyacinth Girl Press in May 2013.

Bekah Steimel's blog interview series, February 19, 2018, "We Surrender Our Dreams to Hunger" (titled here "Mama, Couldn't She Eat a Fly? [Because She Has a Frog Tongue]"); *Fjords Review*, Special Women's Edition (2015), "Mama, What Is Regret?," "Mama, How Does the Woman with the Frog Tongue Eat?," "A Woman, Tempted"; *The Gettysburg Review* 25, no. 2 (Summer 2012), "What Our Mothers Know As Love," "Where Have We Taken Our Husbands And Fathers?"; *Menacing Hedge* 5, no. 2 (Fall 2015), "Chapter I: She Leaves Home," "Chapter II: She is Warned, and Ignores the Warning," "Mama, What Is Regret?," "Mama, How Does the Woman with the Frog Tongue Eat?," "Chapter III: She Cultivates a Harvest She Cannot Reap," "Chapter IV: She Collects Objects That Are Not Hers," "Chapter V: She Discovers What She Desires," "Mama, Where Are Their Parents?"; *Painted Bride Quarterly*, Monsters Issue, no. 95 (2017), "Chapter VI: The Children Have a Request," "Chapter VII: She Grows a Second Heart," "Chapter VIII: She Removes the Stitches," "Chapter IX: The Children Find Her Sleeping"; *Phantom Drift: A Journal of New Fabulism* 7, "Chapter X: How Will This Story End: X.i. Lightning (Transfiguration and Punishment)," "What Our Mothers Won't Name"; *So to Speak: A Feminist Journal of Language and Art* (Spring 2015), "But Mama, Why Do We Remember?"; *The Southern Review* 48, no. 2 (Spring

2012), "Our Mothers Are Children, Too," "The Reason Our Mothers Can't Help Us," "Why Our Mothers Panic"; *Speaking of Marvels*, February 24, 2014, "The Mother Makes Time for Herself"; *Stirring: A Literary Collection*, vol. 16, ed. 4 (April 2014), "A Woman"; *Stirring: A Literary Collection*, vol. 16, ed. 5 (May 2014), "A Woman: Split"; *Verse Daily*, September 21, 2012, "Why Our Mothers Panic" (reprint); *Verse Wisconsin Online*, no. 112 (2013), "A Woman, Addressing Doubt," "The Mistakes Our Mothers Make"

Many thanks and much love to Cynthia Marie Hoffman, Stephanos Papadopoulos, and Adam Penna for invaluable feedback and support of this manuscript in its various stages; to Christian McLean, Julie Sheehan, and the Southampton Writers Conference for the opportunities and resources they have provided over the years; to Dr. J. Bruce Fuller and Lisa Tremaine at Texas Review Press for their enthusiasm and effort on behalf of this book; to Christina Chiu and M.M. De Voe of the nonprofit literary organization Pen Parentis for their kindness to me and important work on behalf of parent-writers; to my own parents, Robert and Elizabeth Kain, my in-laws, Paul and Bertha Gutowski, and my sisters and sisterin-law, Amanda Kain, Katherine Pultz, and AnnaLisa Poio, for their unfailing support as I've navigated academic and writing careers while raising kids. And to Andrew, for being my favorite and my best.